After the Church

Claire Henderson Davis is a freelance writer and artist and co-founder of Public Work (www.publicwork.co.uk), an arts organization and consultancy.

She trained in creative arts and sociology in Montréal and gained a PhD in theology at the University of Edinburgh. She has published numerous articles on contemporary Christian faith and worship in *The Furrow, The Tablet, New Blackfriars, Theology* and *The Observer*. This is her first book.

She lives in London.

After the Church

Divine Encounter in a Sexual Age

Claire Henderson Davis

CANTERBURY
PRESS
Norwich

First published in 2007 by the Canterbury Press Norwich
(a publishing imprint of Hymns Ancient & Modern Limited,
a registered charity)
9–17 St Alban's Place, London N1 0NX

www.scm-canterburypress.co.uk

British Library Cataloguing in Publication data

A catalogue record for this book is available
from the British Library

ISBN 978-1-85311-736-7

Typeset by Regent Typesetting, London
Printed in the UK by CPI Bookmarque, Croydon, CR0 4TD

For the sake of a peace
beyond all understanding

Contents

If the Lover retires too far, the light of love is extinguished and the Beloved dies; if the Lover approaches too near the Beloved, she is effaced by the love and ceases to have an independent existence. The Lovers must leave a distance, a boundary, for love: then they approach and retire so that love may suspire. This may be heard as the economics of Eros; but it may also be taken as the infinite passion of faith.

Gillian Rose
Love's Work, Chatto & Windus, 1995, p. 133

Introduction

My parents left the Roman Catholic Church before I was born. My father was a Roman Catholic priest, my mother a member of The Grail, a lay women's group. My father quit when the Church became an obstacle to holiness, and he wanted a life with my mother beyond its grasp. Their leaving was an act of faith: that God isn't Roman Catholic, and that it's possible to live the good news outside traditional structures. They stopped reading the story and stepped into the book.

I grew up Christian, even Catholic (though I didn't know it at the time), outside the Church. This didn't mean I had no dealings – my father baptized me in the university chaplaincy in Edmonton, where I was born; I was confirmed through my primary school in Montréal, where I grew up; and, like unfaithful lovers, we attended both Roman Catholic and Anglican churches along the way – it meant that I never considered Church the point. It was a useful tool, like training to be an actor: a primer for the stage of life.

The Church though is like a school whose teachers

can't let go, so afraid of what pupils might do on stage, of losing power, that school becomes religion. Performance is abandoned, no one graduates. This distorts the music, for Christianity is not first theory, philosophy, or moral code, but melody, characters joining one note to the next. If no one acts, the plot stagnates, caught in an endless groove. This mix of infantilization and repetition drives out those who dare grow up and sentences the rest to boredom and frustration. Folk outside can't enter unless to surrender an adulthood, hard won in Western, secular democracies. The result is shrinking church attendance and a wider public historically cut off.

But haven't we left Christianity behind? Why keep this story going? A few years ago, a student told me he planned to be a shaman. About 18, of Presbyterian stock (but not church-going) he came from a small town outside Edinburgh, and was typical of undergraduates I met. They were on a search, not just for meaning, but for overt religious practice. Despite nominally Christian backgrounds, they didn't identify with Christianity. It was a relic of the past, at best a boring irrelevance, at worst, a shameful episode. Either way, not a path to explore.

They were profoundly ignorant of the Christian story. They knew the basic, bare bones of the New Testament, and some tales from the Hebrew Bible, but their knowledge was Sunday school. They didn't know the texts, had no grasp of narrative sequence, and no way of relating the story to their lives. They were longing for religion, looking every place but home. Apart from my shaman-hopeful, there were aspiring Buddhists, Hindus and Taoists, devotees of Tarot or crystals, Star Trekkies, and fans of medieval re-enactment. The search for contemporary religious practice is real and widespread: children of dysfunctional transmission, longing for dialogue with God. Like it or not, the West is not comprehensible without Christianity. You can learn other languages, but your mother tongue comes first.

That's not to say there's any easy way of connecting the Christian story to the present. While the West has shifted to democracy, Christian Churches still tolerate parent–child like structures. The result, an enormous gulf between Christian apologia and the street talk of the West. We need words to inform our search for wholeness and integrity, rooted in history, engaged with now, freeing us to act on a more conscious level, to meet the future with greater hope. The West has engaged in an important rebellion against the Church, but in order to mature, we need to reconnect. Not to embrace the Christian cult, but to know where we are in the plot, to take the story forward.

While my peers left the Church by attrition – parents bored but dragging kids along – my own parents left through faith. I have come to see this difference as significant. It prevented them becoming cynical, and after years of schooling, freed them to act their parts. The results were complicated and not uniformly successful. But what emerged was the fruit of real engagement. As this tradition passes to me, I struggle for a language to describe it. In my search, I have studied sociology, and completed a doctorate in theology. I explore liturgical forms through theatre, visual arts and contemporary dance, and myself through Jungian psychoanalysis. Karen Armstrong writes in her *History of God* that 'each generation has to create the image of God that works for them'.[1] This book offers an image of God for my generation, searching for holiness largely outside the Church.

Do I believe in God? My instinct is to follow Moses and hide my face. For Jews it is forbidden to speak or write the name of God, and I share this inhibition. God is unknown and cannot be contained in human language. But language itself speaks of God – not religious language but the sheer factness of expression. We search the edge of language, struggling to say what's not been said. Something within draws us to our limits, and we labour for its name.

Belief in God affirms a reality beyond ourselves which we did not create. We experience our own lives, and human life, within this context – nature, the earth, the universe. We ask questions like: *What are we for? Why are we here? What is our relation to the whole?* Within our known environment, we're the only ones who ask, conscious of life itself, with language our medium.

Language makes us fragile. Passing on the human world, one generation to the next, is not procreation but transmission; communicating where we're at, how we got here, and what's next; keeping track of the story, what it's about.

In the West, the downfall of public narrative is Church

---

1. Karen Armstrong, *A History of God*, London, 1999, p. 5.

control. The world moves on while religion loses touch with language, gets wedded to archaic forms. Stories proliferate as entertainment and escape. Passive congregations turned passive consumers of others' lives, without the means to act. We worship the God of difference, but forget our names.

My story's not entirely my choice – birth, parents, mother tongue. What I do is up to me, but some parameters are given. So with Christianity. It defines our history in ways we can't deny. We identify Christianity with the Church, but they are not identical. The Church as a human institution may collapse, while the story is taken up in other forms. If Christianity has anything more to offer, it's not about being Christian but about being human. I propose to retell the Christian narrative as a story about human life, its limits and how we find them, and our choices when we do. In doing so, I'm trying to bridge the gap between Christian vocabulary and the language of the world at large. The result may resemble a patchwork quilt sewn together with a darning needle. But I hope this inspires others with a talent for finer stitching to try their hand.

When you know a story very well, it can be fascinating to expand the meaning of the blue shirt a lesser character is wearing. To people outside, however, such focus is obscure. One can, in fact, get so enamoured of the blue shirt that the story as a whole is lost. Stories develop layers of accretions, digressions, and dead ends. It can be hard to remember what it's actually about.

I observe a certain grammar about God; the story, at all times, a human tale. This prevents language becoming absolute in the name of divine authority, and keeps the plot moving as new expressions come into play.

The story is also mine: not autobiography so much as exploration of the tension between an individual life, and the social forms which birth it. I write to be free of the story, to claim the future undetermined, finding my way to the limits of the known world in order, there, to greet the unknown. If others find help in what I say, while searching their own locations, it may be as a depth-sounding, or landmark on the map.

1

The Fall

※

On my twenty-fifth birthday, I went to see a psychotherapist. I cried throughout the session, and all I could say was, 'I don't think that I exist.' This curious statement wasn't philosophical reflection or existential angst. It welled up from the depths of my being and seemed the only accurate description of my plight. My story was unravelling; the distance between who I thought I was and reality on the ground, immense. I knew I needed help.

Without our story we are lost. Our individual identity is made up of the story we tell about ourselves, to ourselves and to others; facts woven together in a tapestry of meaning, giving the sense of who we are. My story had become disinformation and propaganda, but without it, I doubted my own existence. If this isn't me, who am I?

Human beings find their place in the world through storytelling. Unlike animals, we have no natural habitat. We create our own belonging by telling the story of how we got here and where we're going. This story links us to a web of human relationship across time and space.

In one sense, my story begins on my twenty-fifth birthday, because it's at this moment that the story I have inherited malfunctions and disintegrates, and I am forced to address the question of who I am from my own resources. At the same time, it begins way back with my parents and grandparents, spanning three countries and deeply marked by the Roman Catholic Church.

Our story is not fixed. It depends on who we're telling – ourselves, a friend, a lover, our mother, our doctor, someone on the bus, all hear different versions of our tale. Also, we're constantly revising it, not only because new things occur, but also because our understanding of the past and our imagining of the future change as we change. At 25, I was to begin retelling my story, radically altering my vision of the world.

My father was a Roman Catholic priest who left the Church in protest against its authoritarian structure, and married my mother, a member of The Grail, a Catholic lay women's movement. For me, this sentence contains everything and nothing. It has so often preceded any account of who I am, yet it says nothing about me and very little about my parents, while setting the scene for my whole life. Telling a story is a difficult task, involving choices about what to include and to discard, what is important and what trivial. The mode of storytelling is also crucial – how to avoid falling into cliché, or being oppressed by dominant categories of meaning, that prevent us really seeing the world.

So I'll begin elsewhere. My mother nearly burned to death when she was three, seated on the back seat of her father's sedan with her three-year-old cousin, Jackie. It

2

happened in minutes, if not seconds – a quick stop for cigarettes, matches left carelessly behind, a flammable dress.

My mother lived her life as though trying to escape from a burning car – she couldn't bear enclosed spaces, or breathe without fresh air. Doors and windows were left open. But it was she, not the car, on fire, and escape eluded her. She felt trapped inside herself, in friendships and conversations – a master of abrupt endings, a woman battling for open space.

I think she mistook marriage for the answer. My father, a Catholic priest escaping from the Church, was her perfect companion in flight. She fled into wifehood, they fled together to Canada, where, in motherhood, she fled the problem of her own life.

Her energy was expurgatory. Nothing stayed inside long enough to be properly digested. She was impulsive, frenetic. Ideas occurred, were implemented or dismissed, as if no time to think. We lived in constant emergency.

In motherhood, her manner was extreme distraction. She could not bear to be in one place, to pay attention, as though jumped out of her own melting skin. I grew into the space this left me, as children do, dizzy with interruptions, aching to be seen. What she saw were chances she had never had, music and ballet lessons, trips to the theatre, private schools. I was the golden child. She escaped into a fantasy of my life, leaving me no way to reach her.

It was the desperation this bequeathed me that broke through at 25, demanding a voice in the story, leaving me speechless.

The stories we tell matter. It's the way we make sense of our lives, know who we are. If we tell false stories that protect us from what we cannot or will not face, we create a false self, disconnected from reality. But reality pursues us, intrudes in unpredictable ways, pressing upon our consciousness. So there's a discipline to storytelling, a struggle to say things truly.

But who's the judge? How do we know if our stories express reality? Surely the answer lies in their effect, the fruit they bear? Weeping in the office of a psychotherapist was at very least a sign to me that the story I had been telling was inadequate. Perhaps another proof has to do with where it leaves us. We describe someone as 'stuck in the past' or 'living for tomorrow', and mean that they're cut off from the present. Imagine a man who hates his job but copes by planning his retirement, or a lonely woman consumed by nostalgia for her childhood. By contrast, a person is described as 'having presence', or 'making their presence felt'. So, in our ordinary speech, we recognize this ability to inhabit time in different ways, and our temptation to escape from now.

Nine months before she died, my mother and I took a trip together to Newfoundland, where her mother and grandmother grew up, descended from a family who emigrated from Ireland in the eighteenth century. She had often told me Newfoundland tales, part of her family lore, but she had never been there herself. They were stories of a cruel and unforgiving life, especially for the women, on a barren, sea-faring island from which her mother had escaped to

New York, followed closely by her mother's mother and seven other children. I thought that if we got to this place, the *ur*-place at the beginning of the story, I might finally get her attention, bind myself to her, not as a fantasy child, but as a daughter, connected through a line of mothers and daughters going back in time.

Although she resisted the meaning of the trip for me, it was an important journey. There was too much pain, and it was too late to begin facing it, but we made enough of a breakthrough to create something real between us.

We are each born at a particular time and place, to particular parents, with a particular language and culture, in a particular society. Before we are even conscious, we have inherited much of what will form our identity. It is then up to us to find our place, to do what we can with these raw materials, to arrive at the present where we, in turn, can make our contribution. What we inherit, however, is not just our belonging, but also our dislocation: stories of hatred and jealousy, injustice and revenge; failures to become conscious; patterns of relationship that obstruct our ability to be present. We inherit the 'original sin' of our forebears and have to struggle, in our own lifetime, to work things out, before handing the world on to our children.

To be in the present, then, is to be connected to, but not dominated by, the past; to be aware of, but not living for, the future. Human beings are not born into the present; getting there is a life's work.

The biblical account of the Fall interprets this cycle of human life as a punishment from God for disobedience.

5

When they eat the forbidden fruit, Adam and Eve become conscious of themselves and their nakedness for the first time, leading to their expulsion from the Garden of Eden. In the course of evolution, what creates a definitive break between human beings and animals is language. Language expels us from the Garden because it makes us conscious of ourselves and the world in a new way. Language creates the ability to imagine a world other than the present, to know that the world has been other in the past, and may be other in the future. It is this ability that gives us our uniquely human place in the world and introduces story-telling as a fundamental feature of human life. Unlike animals, our belonging ceases to be 'natural'. We find our place in a world constructed through language that tells us where we have come from, how we got here and where we are going. We reach the present through our engagement with these stories.

The story of the Fall expresses something fundamental about human life: the grief we feel at our separation from nature, the loss of innocence it brings, the work and suffering required to find our place. This narrative structure may have come to birth at the dawn of human life, when our break from nature was still fresh, but it continues to have power because it expresses an ongoing human experience. All of us, in a sense, are banished from the Garden of Eden at birth, and into a world structured in human terms, which separates us from our home in mother's womb. We are cast out into a life of work and struggle no matter how happy our childhood, and cannot escape the task of finding our own place. The Fall also describes moments throughout our life when we experience a loss of innocence as a new level of consciousness takes hold, and we are forced to question things that once we took for granted, challenging our vision of the world. Sitting in the psychotherapist's office on my twenty-fifth birthday was, for me, an instance of the Fall.

The Fall is a story grounded in real human experience, a way of making sense of the cycle of human life. We might decide, from our perspective today, that we wouldn't describe this cycle in terms of punishment or disobedience, or that we reject the blame attributed to Eve, and the misogyny it reveals, but we still recognize the human reality addressed, if framed in different terms:

Now the serpent was more subtle than any other wild creature that the Lord God had made.

He said to the woman, 'Did God say, "You shall not eat of any tree of the garden"?' And the woman said to the serpent, 'We may eat of the fruit of the trees of the garden; but God said, "You shall not eat of the fruit of the tree which is in the midst of the garden, neither shall you touch it, lest you die."' But the serpent said to the woman, 'You will not die. For God knows that when you eat of it you will be like God, knowing good and evil.' So when the woman saw that the tree was good for food, and that it was a delight to the eyes, and that the tree was to be desired to make one wise, she took of its fruit and ate; and she also gave some to her husband, and he ate.

7

Then the eyes of both were opened, and they knew that they were naked; and they sewed fig leaves together and made themselves aprons.

And they heard the sound of the Lord God walking in the garden in the cool of the day, and the man and his wife hid themselves from the presence of the Lord God among the trees of the garden. But the Lord God called to the man, and said to him, 'Where are you?' And he said, 'I heard the sound of thee in the garden, and I was afraid, because I was naked; and I hid myself.' He said, 'Who told you that you were naked? Have you eaten of the tree of which I commanded you not to eat?' The man said, 'The woman whom thou gavest to be with me, she gave me fruit of the tree, and I ate.' Then the Lord God said to the woman, 'What is this that you have done?' The woman said, 'The serpent beguiled me, and I ate.' The Lord God said to the serpent,

'Because you have done this,
     cursed are you above all cattle,
   and above all wild animals;
upon your belly you shall go,
     and dust you shall eat
   all the days of your life.
I will put enmity between you and the woman,
     and between your seed and her seed;
he shall bruise your head,
     and you shall bruise his heel.'

To the woman he said,

> 'I will greatly multiply your pain in childbearing;
> > in pain you shall bring forth children,
> yet your desire shall be for your husband,
> > and he shall rule over you.'

And to Adam he said,

> 'Because you have listened to the voice of your wife,
> > and have eaten of the tree
> of which I commanded you,
> > "You shall not eat of it,"
> cursed is the ground because of you;
> > in toil you shall eat of it all the days of your life;
> thorns and thistles it shall bring forth to you;
> > and you shall eat the plants of the field.
> In the sweat of your face
> > you shall eat bread
> till you return to the ground,
> > for out of it you were taken
> you are dust,
> > and to dust you shall return.'

Genesis 3.1–19

The debate between creation and evolution, as two alternative and competing accounts of the world, is nonsense, a mistake about language. The stories of creation and the Garden of Eden are the fruit of human attempts to understand the world, and the place of human life within it. The discovery of evolution transforms this understanding, and therefore our imaginations. But the story of the Garden of Eden continues to have power, not because backward religionists refuse to obey the voice of reason, but because it is a story arising out of and expressing a lived human experience. Human beings did evolve out of a unity with nature, and through language develop a unique relationship with their environment. Throughout our lives we repeat the experience of leaving the Garden as we leave our mother, our home, our job, our country, our taken-for-granted assumptions to make our own way in the world.

Insisting on a literal reading of the story eliminates the narrative flexibility necessary to tell it in the context of a changing world. But imagining that the language of evolution eliminates the need for narrative is just as blind and ignorant.

We experience our agency as human beings at a narrative level. I act within the framework of a story passed on to me, and constructed by me, which tells me who I am and what I am about. This story grows and develops as I engage with the world. I may experience moments of dramatic change or even collapse as aspects of reality intrude which cannot be contained within the story's present structure. Such disintegration may entail a loss of identity, as parts of the story are left behind, but, ultimately, such moments call us towards greater maturity – towards an expansion of the story to embrace what could not previously be named.

If I hang on to a literal reading of the story as a direct communication from God, a bulwark against all change, I cut myself off from the possibility of real engagement, from encounter with the unknown and the other, from which my story protects me. If I believe that processes are at work, revealed by science, which determine the course of my life regardless of the narrative level at which I pitch my own agency, this equally protects me from the vulnerability and risk involved in making real choices that matter.

How can we tell our stories in ways that remain open to each other and the world, and our changing understanding of both? Today, this is a life and death question on whose answer the future of the world may rest.

2

Babel to Pentecost

ॐ

I don't find it hard to understand why young Muslims are attracted to martyrdom, or to imagine the story that posits 9/11 as a victory in a holy war. Growing up with Catholic martyrology, and its accounts of gruesome ends met by saints remaining true to faith, the idea of dying in a holy cause is certainly familiar. On top of this, the crusades and the inquisition offer ample precedent for slaughtering others on behalf of God. The attraction of a cause that asks you to lay down your life for a higher good can be immense, lifting you out of the concerns of daily life, and into an intensity of meaning, which suddenly bestows importance. Being part of an alternative social structure, which provides belonging, when belonging is hard to find, is also a big draw. It dignifies the role of outsider, trans-forming rejection into opposition, creating disciples of a better way.

The mantle of outsider runs through my family, and although we haven't turned to violent revolution, that's probably circumstantial. My mother grew up in an immi-grant neighbourhood of Brooklyn, New York in the 1930s and 40s, and so strong was her identity as a Catholic that she didn't fully realize she was also American until John F. Kennedy, a fellow Catholic, became President. My father grew up in Britain, where the Roman Catholic Church retained its outsider mentality from penal times. For both my parents, the Church provided a path out of their working-class backgrounds into education, and into contact with a wider social spectrum. I, in turn, was raised a child of immigrants in French Canada, with parents who couldn't speak the language. Although we lived in an English enclave, I attended mainly French schools, and despaired at the gulf between my home life and the world outside.

We live at a time when the search for identity is acute, and particular identities are vigorously asserted all over the world. At the same time, the hegemonizing force of globalization is everywhere at work. The clash between Western democracies and radical Islam highlights the tension created by these different trends. The creed of Western democracy is that public space remains a neutral ground. Individuals are free to pursue particular interests and identities, including religion, in private, and these differences may even be publicly celebrated, but the public ordering of society remains impartial. What happens when this creed comes up against radical Islam, whose adherents want to make a substantive impact on public space, to create a society pleasing to God?

For twenty years, my mother was a member of The Grail, a movement of lay Catholic women whose mission was to convert the world for Christ. They trained young Catholic women on a farm in Ohio, preparing them for marriage and leadership roles in the Church, and in their local communities. Their aim was certainly to influence public space, and they went about it in both open and covert ways. They followed a rigorous personal discipline, keeping the observances of the Church, and submitting to intimate scrutiny of their lives. They were sent out into the world as witnesses, taking secular jobs which provided occasion, through example, to attract others to the path. My mother, at one point, worked as a waitress in a restaurant where the boss instituted a competition, offering a free steak to the employee who, during the week, sold the most steak dinners, the most expensive item on the menu. My mother won, but the boss told her she would have to eat her steak on Friday. As a good Catholic, this was impossible, and she declined. The boss, impressed by her devotion, relented. A fellow-conspirator worked in the post office, where, every day at noon, she knelt down and said the Angelus, a prayer traditionally said by Catholics at midday. These are only small examples of The Grail's elaborate strategy of 'infil-tration', a word they used themselves.

My father's approach, even as a priest, was more intel-lectual, taking the form of writing and teaching, but he too bore public witness, at Speaker's Corner in Hyde Park, for example, on behalf of the Catholic Truth Society.

Although, in their lifetime, they travelled far, and came to reject this earlier position, my parents certainly, at one stage, believed that the Roman Catholic Church was in sole possession of the truth, and that it was incumbent upon them, as faithful and active members, to convey this truth to the rest of the world. The fact that they did not take up arms in this cause seems to me purely a matter of historical chance. If they had lived at a time when violent witness was required, I am sure the certainty of their conviction would have carried them along.

Surely the promise of democracy is the promise of a conversation between adults about how to live together in society, which addresses substantive questions of value. The idea that people are entitled to their private beliefs, as long as these do not impinge on public space, maintains the illusion that public space is, in fact, a neutral ground. One has only to walk through any Western city to see that this is not the case, every inch of public space consumed by advertising, proclaiming the creed of Western capitalist societies that every decision can be reduced to consumer choice.

Western democracy is indeed based on substantive values – freedom of the individual, freedom of speech, freedom of the press, universal franchise, an independent judiciary, and equality before the law. In theory, we are free to conduct any conversation we choose about the ordering of our society. In practice, this conversation is corrupted by the use of public space to promote private interests, in the shape of advertising, which masquerades as stories about human fulfilment, while impeding our ability to explore together what human fulfilment really looks like.

The problem with advertising is that it cynically addresses our desire for fulfilment with promises it cannot keep. It creates a vision of a better world, but offers a path that doesn't go there. So what? Who actually believes that 'Coke is it', or that the Venus razor will 'reveal the Goddess in you', that 'summer starts' at McDonald's, or that KFC is 'the perfect way to end a family day'? However in control we imagine we are in relation to the way advertising affects us, and to how we make decisions about what to buy, revenues prove that we are ensnared in its seductions. Advertising works.

It works by actively shaping our individual and collective imaginations, holding before us the things we most desire – love, sex, relationship, family, pleasure, success, health, beauty – tantalizing us with promises of delivery. But, delivery never comes, because in advertising there is no actual relationship between the path and the destination – cleaning products do not deliver happy family life – so the underlying message is that there is no real fulfilment, nothing works.

We are encouraged to believe that ultimately this system benefits everyone, because the more we buy, the more jobs and wealth we create, the faster the economy grows, and the sooner everyone gets a piece of the pie. But the vacuum of meaning generated is vast. The search for meaning, reduced to a private quest, takes off in all directions. In the absence of any collective narrative able to create shared meaning, people desperately cling to particular identities. At the same time, there is general apathy, a lack of faith in politicians, and a lack of participation in the democratic process. Many people seem no longer to believe in the possibility of social change.

Human fulfilment is a story, as advertisers well know, about the shape of what we hope for, and where we are going, about transformation and change. We can only tell this story effectively to the extent that we can both imagine the world other than it is now, and act to make it so. Advertising corrupts this ability by creating a disconnect between our imagination of a better world, and the action required to bring it about. True worth is not delivered by L'Oréal.

The world today can be characterized in terms of a struggle between particular identities on the one hand, many in violent conflict with each other, and globalization on the other, fuelled by Western capitalist economies, based on the promise of wealth through consumer culture. Because consumerism, however, offers no substantive vision of human fulfilment, it cannot act as arbiter between different and opposing points of view. Its deepest counsel is salvation through shopping.

The dominant theory in the field of human evolution is that *Homo sapiens* evolved in Africa then spread out across the globe. In other words, an original unity was followed by increasing difference between human populations – different languages and cultures, different forms of society. These differences have, throughout human history, been the cause of conflict and war. We find a story about this original unity, and its dispersion, in the biblical tale of the Tower of Babel. In this story, human beings, united by one language, try to build a tower that reaches into heaven, rivalling God. As punishment for their arrogance, God confuses their language and scatters them over the earth:

Now the whole earth had one language and few words. And as men migrated from the east, they found a plain in the land of Shinar and settled there. And they said to one another, 'Come, let us make bricks, and burn them thoroughly.' And they had brick for stone, and bitumen for mortar. Then they said, 'Come, let us build ourselves a city, and a tower with its top in the heavens, and let us make a name for ourselves, lest we be scattered abroad upon the face of the whole earth.' And the Lord came down to see the city and the tower, which the sons of men had built. And the Lord said, 'Behold, they are one people, and they have all one language; and this is only the beginning of what they will do; and nothing that they propose to do will now be impossible for them. Come, let us go down, and there confuse their language, that they may not understand one another's speech.' So the Lord scattered them abroad from there over the face of all the earth, and they left off building the city. Therefore its name was called Ba'bel, because there the Lord confused the language of all the earth; and from there the Lord scattered them abroad over the face of all the earth.
Genesis 11.1–9

With all the conflict that ensued, it's no wonder this account of difference took shape as a narrative of punishment. This story, however, is relevant, not only to the beginning of human life, but to our ongoing temptation to eliminate difference by imposing a single language; the seduction of an undifferentiated unity. There are count-

18

less examples throughout history: the Roman Empire, the Catholic Church, colonialism, Nazi Germany, the Soviet Union, Greater Serbia, the globalization of Western capitalism.

What is the alternative to a unity achieved through eradicating difference? Is the only solution a truce-like state, keeping differences apart and private in the name of a neutral public order? Or is it possible we might discover a process of engagement able to create a real and substantive unity without eliminating difference?

There is a story in the Christian New Testament which provides a vision of such unity: After Jesus' death, his disciples are gathered together in a house, trying to work out what to do next. The Holy Spirit, we are told, descends on them in tongues of fire, enabling them to tell the story of Jesus to the crowd outside, so that each person hears it in their own language. The great breakthrough Jesus makes is to see that salvation is not for the Jews alone, that God's love extends equally to all people across differences in language, race, culture, creed, sex and social status. Certainly Christian churches have frequently, if not mostly, read this story as an imperative to impose Christianity on the world, but this is not the only, or perhaps the best, interpretation. The word spoken to the crowd creates unity, but without imposing a single language; differences flourish in relation to a word that brings news of acceptance and the promise of peace:

When the day of Pentecost had come, they were all

together in one place. And suddenly a sound came from heaven like the rush of a mighty wind, and it filled all the house where they were sitting. And there appeared to them tongues as of fire, distributed and resting on each one of them. And they were all filled with the Holy Spirit and began to speak in other tongues, as the Spirit gave them utterance.

Now there were dwelling in Jerusalem Jews, devout men from every nation under heaven. And at this sound the multitude came together, and they were bewildered, because each one heard them speaking in his own language. And they were amazed and wondered, saying, 'Are not all these who are speaking Galileans? And how is it that we hear, each of us in his own native language? Parthians and Medes and Elamites and residents of Mesopotamia, Judea and Cappadocia, Pontus and Asia, Phrygia and Pamphylia, Egypt and the parts of Libya belonging to Cyrene, and visitors from Rome, both Jews and proselytes, Cretans and Arabians, we hear them telling in our own tongues the mighty works of God.'
Acts 2.1–11

The West, in its current form, has developed out of the view that our stories are what divide us, and that reason is the only basis for social unity. Different leaders come together to discuss 'issues', 'values', and 'morality', leaving stories out of the public sphere through faith that rational discussion will create common space where narrative remains sectarian. On an individual level, however, the opposite is true. Public space is full of personal stories, from the voyeurism of *Big Brother* to the epic of Nelson Mandela's life. Our thirst for narrative is sated through tales of individual lives, but our longing for participation in collective narrative remains unmet.

Our fear of collective narrative is well founded – Fascism and Church control are fresh memories, and the battle of opposing stories, even today, is alive and well throughout the world.

But do we not kid ourselves imagining that rationality is the driving force in Western secular democracies? Are we not just ignoring the form that public narrative is taking, and therefore failing to take account of its power and influence, unable to make conscious decisions about its role?

Advertisers take up the space of public narrative with their pseudo-tales of human fulfilment, catering to purely private interests. At the other extreme, the nightly news presents the story of the world each day, as though from a place of disinterested impartiality. On the one hand, fulfilment always beyond our reach; on the other, hard reality we seemingly cannot change. Into the void created by this split come narratives of transformation.

The astounding success of books like the *Harry Potter* series and *The Da Vinci Code*, coupled with the popularity of reality television, bear witness to a collective longing, crying out for attention. Both *Harry Potter* and *The Da Vinci Code* provide accounts of a world within the world as it now appears – a world you might find if you only know how to look. Both, in completely different ways, make the connection between the ordinary world, and a world of extraordinary intensity and meaning.

Reality television does a similar thing by showing us the transformation of a person's life through a controlled process or situation – cooking, making the dog behave, making the children behave, living in the jungle, living in a house, living in a monastery or convent, having a makeover, learning how to dress or dance or sing. All these programmes, however trivial, take us on a journey with the participants, allowing us to watch as people's lives are changed.

The desire that fuels the popularity of these books and shows is at the root of all religious practice – desire for a life and world transformed, for intensity of meaning and purpose, for a connectedness that moves us beyond the ordinary and the mundane.

I remember coming across an interview with J. K. Rowling, the author of *Harry Potter*, in which a young fan asks her, 'Do you really believe in magic?' Rowling gently replies that she does not. However wonderful the *Harry Potter* books, they cannot substitute for a real public narrative that charts a path from our present location (the news) to a world transformed (the ads), because this kind of narrative must be both historical and imaginative – describing the world as it really is while offering a vision of what it might become. In order to find this path, we need to begin by re-discovering the connection between word and flesh.

3

Incarnation

৪৯

When I was sixteen, my father took a sabbatical year from his university teaching post in Montréal, and we went to live at a theological research institute on the West Bank, between Jerusalem and Bethlehem. There, I met an American student, ten years older than I, who, over the course of the year, became my first boyfriend.

My parents grew up with strict Catholic teaching on sex – sex was only ever permissible between a married heterosexual couple, and contraception, apart from the rhythm method, forbidden. Each had spent 20 years in Catholic institutions, my father as a priest, my mother, a member of The Grail. When they married at ages 44 and 39, both were virgins.

Although able to talk openly about sex on a theoretical level, in practice, they remained surprisingly conservative. This created a context in which having sex with my boyfriend, to whom I was neither married nor engaged, nor likely to be in the near future, was inconceivable.

Today, my parents' approach seems bizarrely old-fashioned, but I wonder, on a deep level, how far the situation has changed. Reports of teenage sex in the media seem invariably negative, focusing on high rates of teenage pregnancy and the threat of sexually transmitted disease. What seems lacking is any positive account of young people's initiation into sexual activity. While the sexual revolution successfully discarded a lot of baggage, it seems we are still struggling to express a new vision of sex, relevant to contemporary life. Christianity may seem the last place to look for such a vision, but perhaps it's worth exploring where we've come from in trying to work this out.

Sexual difference is fundamental to both human and animal life, the structure of procreation. In the human world, however, this difference takes on meaning transcending pure physicality; the position of men and women in sexual intercourse relates to accepted positions in society. On this basis, men have been characterized as active and penetrating, women, passive and open, waiting to receive. In Christianity, incarnation, the word of God becoming flesh in the person of Jesus, can be read in terms of a hierarchy of sexual difference. God approaches Mary, through the angel Gabriel, telling her that she has been chosen to bear his son. She submits to God's will and is penetrated by the Holy Spirit, conceiving Jesus:

In the sixth month the angel Gabriel was sent from God to a city of Galilee named Nazareth, to a virgin betrothed to a man whose name was Joseph, of the House of David; and the virgin's name was Mary. And he came to her and said, 'Hail, O favoured one, the Lord is with you!' But she was greatly troubled at the saying, and considered in her mind what sort of greeting this might be. And the angel said to her, 'Do not be afraid, Mary, for you have found favour with God. And behold, you will conceive in your womb and bear a son, and you shall call his name Jesus.

He will be great, and will be called
the Son of the Most High;
and the Lord God will give to him
the throne of his father David,
and he will reign over the house of
Jacob for ever;
and of his kingdom there will be no end.'

And Mary said to the angel, 'How shall this be, since I have no husband?' And the angel said to her,

'The Holy Spirit will come upon you,
and the power of the Most High
will overshadow you;
therefore the child to be born
will be called holy,
the Son of God.'

Luke 1.26–35

In this story, God enters the human world by adopting a male sexual position, impregnating Mary, who bears his son. In relation to God, the human world is female – open, receptive, waiting for God's word to penetrate, but also, sinful and fallen, needing to be saved. In relation to Jesus, God's son, the Church is also female, 'the bride of Christ', his partner in bringing about the world's salvation. In this hierarchy of sexual difference, men, who share the sexual position of God, in relation to women, are closer to God's perfection than women, who share the sexual position of the sinful and fallen world. Men are closer to the word, women to the flesh.

This dichotomy underpinned a whole history of oppression and subjugation of women, challenged in our own time through the feminist movement. But the story doesn't end here. The extraordinary success of Dan Brown's novel, *The Da Vinci Code*, gives some insight into the continuing power of this narrative, and our need to retell it, in light of the contemporary context.

Dan Brown takes the character of Mary Magdalene, a follower of Jesus, traditionally portrayed by the Church as a prostitute, and puts her, alongside him, at the centre of the story. In Brown's retelling, Mary Magdalene is Jesus' wife and equal, royal in her own right. She is the one commissioned by Jesus to lead his Church. When he is crucified, she is pregnant with their child, and flees to France, where the child, a daughter, is born. The subsequent history of Christianity is described in terms of a massive cover-up by a male-dominated Church, desperate to suppress this feminine aspect of God's revelation.

Discussions of this book have focused almost exclusively on whether or not it is literally true, ignoring its possible function at other levels of the collective imagination. What it suggests is that there is a feminine aspect of God, equal to the masculine, and essential to any balanced vision of human wholeness. Sex is at the heart of this vision; God's incarnation, the fruit of sexual intercourse between equal partners.

What is certainly 'true' in this account is that we are emerging from a long history of sexual oppression, aided and abetted by the Church, and characterized by a fundamentalist account of sexual difference, positioning men above women, and masculine attributes above feminine ones. The astonishing success of *The Da Vinci Code*, if taken seriously, reveals the need and desire for a narrative of sexual equality to shape the space in which such equality can be lived in human terms.

Before their engagement, my parents had never touched each other in an intimate way, or even discussed their relationship in intimate terms. On one level, this is simply because my father was a priest, faithful to his vow of celibacy, but their situation was not unique among Catholics. My mother described a friend who was about to be married. So lofty and spiritual were her friend's ideas about married life, that the day before the wedding her husband-to-be asked, 'You do realize there's a physical side to marriage?'

My father proposed to my mother in a letter, and my mother accepted by post. At their next meeting, faced with each other for the first time on these new terms, they had very different expectations. They met at my mother's flat. She had made a beautiful meal and taken great care in her attire. She expected them to begin a gradual process of *rapprochement*, but when my father arrived, the first thing he said was, 'Aren't you going to kiss me?'

For my mother, this was a disaster, shattering her fantasy

27

of what their life was to be. From today's perspective, I wonder why she didn't just say, 'I'm not ready to kiss you yet, let's have dinner first', but she had no language to talk about her own needs and desires.

In a conversation between two people, both partners alternate between the masculine and feminine position. When I talk, I am masculine, sending my words into my partner, who is feminine, listening and taking them in. When she, in turn, speaks, she is masculine, and I, feminine. If our conversation is fertile, we create something new between us in language, the child of our exchange. The masculine and feminine positions are complementary, interdependent and equal, not identified exclusively with either men or women, because both assume both roles. We all know the stereotype of the man who can't listen, or the woman too timid to speak, but neither make good conversation.

My mother's problem was that, from her position, she felt unable to speak. Her formation identified her, as a woman, exclusively with a feminine role, so she was unable to communicate her situation to my father, or even become fully aware of it herself. As a result, she felt oppressed and put off by his desires. This situation continued throughout their marriage, and meant that they never found sexual fulfilment with each other. My mother resorted to indirect communication through manipulation, emotional pressure and even illness, but she never found the language to express her needs in an open and direct way.

My father, for his part, took my mother's consent for

granted, and since she never challenged him, he was able to persist in the fantasy that their needs and desires were identical. When he proposed, he failed to mention his intention to leave the Roman Catholic Church, which had been my mother's whole life, and simply assumed she would follow his decision. There was no question that my father's career would take precedence in their marriage. In the story of the incarnation, Mary's virtue lies in her virginity, and submission to God's will. This was the model of womanhood held before my mother.

Virginity indicates that a woman has no sexual history, she is a blank page waiting to be filled. This ideal of feminine virginity has implications, not only for women, but for the feminine position in conversation and creative life, which applies equally to men.

Incarnation, the idea that 'word' becomes 'flesh', is a language we may not use in our ordinary lives, but it describes a creative process with which we are all familiar. Making anything, in the human world, involves two different aspects, the 'word' aspect – imagining the thing I want to make, developing an idea, coming up with a plan – and the 'flesh' aspect – engaging my imagination with the materials I want to use, putting the idea into practice, executing the plan. The final result will depend on the form of relationship that pertains between these two different stages of my making.

Like a conversation, the exchange is sexual – the 'word' aspect is masculine, and the 'flesh', feminine: my idea penetrates and impregnates the material world in some form or another, and in its womb, the idea is embodied, taking a particular shape. This relationship can go wrong in different ways: We describe someone as an 'armchair anthropologist' who has no experience on the ground. Public sector workers get angry when the government imposes its plans without acknowledging their experience and expertise at delivering services to the public. We describe people as having their head in the clouds or stuck in an ivory tower. When things go wrong from this direction, we talk of ideas disconnected from reality, not grounded in experience or based on fact. This happens when an assumption of virginity is made, when I seek to impose my ideas without considering the history, experience and wisdom of the embodied reality before me, when I imagine I can have my way without entering into conversation.

At the other extreme, we encounter projects which are not thought through enough, not adequately planned, simply wasting resources. We describe a person as thoughtless or brainless, who doesn't reflect on their actions, but simply ploughs ahead. Here also, there is a failure of conversation between word and flesh.

So we have a sense, even if we do not use this language, that good outcomes are the product of good sex, a creative interaction between word and flesh, based on the equality, autonomy and integrity of each aspect which, when successful, brings forth a new creation.

This account of sex, using the language of conversation and incarnation, distinguishes masculine and feminine positions and roles, without identifying these exclusively with men or women. In this interpretation, real creativity requires a balance of masculine and feminine within each person, as well as between partners. Think of someone with great ideas, who never gets anything done, or a person so wedded to routine that any new idea is a threat. The interaction of word and flesh is both internal and external.

This vision of sex embraces both heterosexual and homosexual partnership. If masculine and feminine aspects of being are found in different combinations within each person, then sexual attraction is necessarily diverse. We are drawn to the particular sexual make-up of another, not simply to their physical constitution as man or woman.

Sex, understood in these terms, is the form of human creativity as well as of procreation. Just as a baby has the genes of both father and mother, and yet is a new and unique person, so too does the product of sexual exchange in conversation and creative work contain the DNA of all participants, while, at the same time, embodying something new.

Advertising works by selling us visions of a world transformed. We are invited to imagine ourselves thinner, fitter, more beautiful, happier, healthier, protected and loved, successful, hip, popular, fulfilled, but the products that purportedly lead to these visions, in fact, bear no inherent relationship to the visions themselves. There is no connection in advertising between word and flesh. Air fresheners don't lead to a happy home. Despite apparent sexiness, there is no sex.

Incarnation, as a description of human creative life,

doesn't offer any immediate picture of the end result. It invites us to engage in a particular form of relationship with each other and the material world, and by respecting the process of this relationship, the form of the new creation is gradually uncovered.

If I am about to undertake a project, I will have some worked-out idea of what the project is about – a plan, a budget, a set of aims and objectives. But the project is not simply the application of my plan. As I actually embark on it, I learn new things which alter my idea. I see that I have underestimated certain costs, or have failed to include unforeseen costs. Certain things I planned don't work well, and I need to adjust. Or other things are more successful than I anticipated and need expansion. A successful outcome is the product of creative interaction between my idea and the work involved in bringing it to fruition. In that process, my vision itself changes, grows, develops and matures, as I engage with the limits and constraints, as well as the possibilities, of material reality.

So it is when I enter into relationship with another person. I have some idea of what the relationship is about, and who the other person is. As I engage in a process of sexual exchange, my fantasies may be shattered and my projections revealed. If the relationship is to develop, therefore, my vision will have to grow and change, as I encounter the reality before me. The relationship we build together will be the fruit of this exchange, but I don't know in advance what it will look like.

If we leave young people at the mercy of advertising and

the popular media, then good sex seems dependent on large breasts, thin bodies, toned muscles, fashionable clothes, and good technique. There is no mystery involved in this vision of sex, no sense of entering a process of encounter with another, whose outcome is unknown.

I came to regret not having sex with my first boyfriend at sixteen, although I'm not sure I could have acted differently. Not only were my parents conservative, I was also living on the West Bank with no independent access to contraception. When we first arrived, the Palestinian staff advised my parents that, for my own safety, I should not be allowed out alone. Although I didn't abide by this instruction, my independence was limited. It was not an ideal environment to assert my sexual freedom.

But the problem was deeper still: I had no narrative of sexual initiation available to me, that didn't involve engagement and marriage as a prescribed ending; no account of sex as an open-ended process of encounter.

Not having sex, the next step in this unfolding intimacy, tied me in knots for years to come. I found it hard to imagine sex with someone else, when it had been impossible with a person I had grown to love. Eventually, I felt I simply had to overcome this obstacle, and had sex with a man I danced with in a club. It helped me to move on, but wasn't the initiation it might have been.

4

The Trinity

⚘

Eventually, I moved from psychotherapy to Jungian psycho-analysis. At one of our first sessions, I was telling my analyst about having worked as an auxiliary nurse for a year, after my father's death. She said, 'You did nursing because you needed to be nursed' (she meant breastfed).

At the time, I thought she was bonkers – it seemed such a simplistic interpretation, a cartoon parody of the psycho-analytic exchange. I found it hard to imagine my psyche so mistaking one thing for another, without my knowledge.

It's easy to imagine that we know ourselves, have direct access to the contents of our inner world, and need only decide what to communicate to others. This view creates the impression that, without such a decision, no one else knows what's going on inside; that the body, a barrier hold-ing things in, is only crossed through a conscious act of will.

At a common sense level, we know this to be false. We read a great deal from how people look, the clothes they wear, their facial expressions and body language, quite apart from what they say. We tell a lot about someone simply by observing them. Even when a person speaks, we often read a subtext below the level of the words. We pick up when, 'Would you like some more coffee?' means, 'It's time to go'. Far from a barrier, holding our true selves in, the body is a powerful medium of expression, never entirely within our conscious control. We speak despite ourselves.

To become self-aware, then, is not to start from scratch, but to develop conscious knowledge of patterns of communication already at work both within ourselves, and in relation to others. As we become more conscious of what and how we communicate, an arena of choice opens up, not available before. We become agents of our actions in a new way. If I go into nursing because I am looking to be nursed, I will be disappointed, just as when we eat to satisfy hunger that has nothing to do with food. By becoming conscious of my need, I gain the freedom and choice to address it more directly, and the hope that it can, in some form, be met.

We participate in patterns of communication not original to us, beginning with our parents, or going back generations in our family, and extending beyond our family circle to our particular society and time. So, in a very real sense, discovering who we are is not only an internal work, moving from the inside out, but also a work of external enquiry, discovering ourselves from the outside in.

When we refer to the body, then, we are describing not an inert physical mass, or material appendage, but the location and medium of all our communicative activity, a hub of relationality, connecting the different parts of us internally, and our self to the rest of the world. Our body is formed at levels beyond our conscious control, communicating both to us and others in ways of which we are often unaware. We are not first and foremost individuals struggling to communicate, but products of particular social patterning, acting out forms of communication and relationship we have been taught. Our body has a history not solely of our making.

Psychotherapy investigates the body's history predominantly on a personal level, but the social level is no less important. Where do certain patterns of relationality come from, which produce individual body types dominant in a given age? We identify this relationship between the individual and social bodies when, for example, we describe someone as a 'Victorian' or a 'Thatcherite', meaning that they individually express a particular social pattern. Understanding the social level is critical because possibilities for individual development are, in important respects, limited by dominant social forms.

In contemporary Western society, the individual, it might be argued, is the dominant social form. The self has become the primary location of meaning for us. We are not motivated by political ideology or religious authority so much as by the search for individual fulfilment. But what does such fulfilment look like?

There are images all around us of the kind of body we ought to have – young, slender, beautiful, fit and healthy. These images portray an object to be groomed and manicured, not a subject engaged in patterns of communication. Surrounded by such images, it's difficult to imagine another approach to body beautiful, the vision of a person able to relate in certain ways.

Depth psychology provides a language of human wholeness in which relationship is central. Human development is described in terms of a series of relationships, which build the foundations of the self, those with mother and father being primary. Is this language only relevant to the individual, however, or might we use it to help us understand the social body as well?

The Christian Church came to the conclusion that God must be described as three persons in one, that God is fundamentally a pattern of relationship between persons, and within a single person. Considered through the framework of depth psychology, this looks remarkably like a contemporary picture of the self, as both the pattern of relationship within, between different parts of a person, and without, between different people. Using this language to revisit the tradition, it's possible to read the emergence of the individual as the latest stage in a developing narrative, driven by the human search for wholeness. Through this prism, the narrative actually begins prior to the traditional beginning of the story, and relates to what is initially rejected.

In the course of human development, the first relationship we have is with our mother. To begin with, a baby relates only to her mother's breast, and is not aware of the mother as a separate person. The world gets divided into the good and bad breast. The good breast arrives when the baby needs it, the bad breast doesn't come on time and causes, in its absence, unbearable feelings. Gradually the baby becomes able to apprehend the mother as another person, and to integrate the good and bad feelings as both relating to her.

Our relationship with our mother begins in bodily union, and moves towards separation. We look to our mother for the total provision of our bodily needs. She holds us in her arms, and feeds us at her breast, but this holding and feeding also constitute an exchange which begins the process of bringing the baby into the human, linguistic world. A baby is full of strong, passionate feelings of love, hate, despair, rage, joy, which she is not capable of digesting on her own. Just as the mother feeds the baby at the breast, so the baby projects these powerful feelings into the mother, who digests them and gives them back in manageable form. So the baby has the experience of being heard, held, contained and the world made safe.

We can relate this stage of human development to our first imagining of God as a god of nature, mother earth. Humans look to this God to meet their most basic human needs – to make the crops grow, protect them from drought and other natural disasters, keep them safe in the world. Nature is both the good and bad breast, bringing both abundance and suffering. Human beings are relatively powerless in relation to this God, there is little we can do to alter nature's course. At the same time, people look to her, as to a mother, to contain all the powerful, passionate forces in human life, not easily digested. These are presented in the form of sacrifices offered for her consumption. So this first imagining of God is of a god of nature, who reveals herself via cycles and events in the natural world, and is worshipped through sacrifice. This is the God at the beginning of our story, the pagan fertility god, but our story actually begins as a movement away from this God.

A young baby is less aware of her father. For a considerable period of time, the father plays a background role in the life of the baby. The baby is completely absorbed in the mother. Eventually, however, she becomes able to tolerate a third person in the relationship, and the father begins to have a greater place in the child's life. While the mother's role can be described as holding, the father represents the world outside mother's arms, and his role lies in establishing its rules and boundaries. Through the father, the child begins to establish contact with the adult world.

Our story begins as a shift from sacrifice to obedience as the form of worship of this new God. We see the beginning of this shift in the story of Abraham and Isaac:

After these things God tested Abraham, and said to him, 'Abraham!' And he said, 'Here am I.' He said, 'Take your son, your only son Isaac, whom you love, and go to the land of Moriah, and offer him there as a burnt offering upon one of the mountains of which I shall tell you.' So Abraham rose early in the morning, saddled his ass, and took two of his young men with him, and his son Isaac; and he cut the wood for the burnt offering, and arose and went to the place of which God had told him. On the third day Abraham lifted up his eyes and saw the place afar off. Then Abraham said to his young men, 'Stay here with the ass; I and the lad will go yonder and worship, and come again to you.' And Abraham took the wood of the burnt offering, and laid it on Isaac his son; and he took in his hand the fire and the knife. So they went both of them together. And Isaac said to his father Abraham, 'My father!' And he said, 'Here am I, my son.' He said, 'Behold, the fire and the wood; but where is the lamb for a burnt offering?' Abraham said, 'God will provide himself the lamb for a burnt offering, my son.' So they went both of them together.

When they came to the place of which God had told him, Abraham built an altar there, and laid the wood in order, and bound Isaac his son, and laid him on the altar, upon the wood. Then Abraham put forth his hand, and took the knife to slay his son. But the angel of the Lord called to him from heaven, and said, 'Abraham, Abraham!' And he said, 'Here am I.' He said, 'Do not lay your hand on the lad or do anything to him; for now I know that you fear God, seeing you have not withheld your son, your only son, from me.' And Abraham lifted up his eyes and looked, and behold, behind him was a ram, caught in a thicket by his horns; and Abraham went and took the ram, and offered it up as a burnt offering instead of his son. So Abraham called the name of that place The Lord will provide; as it is said to this day, 'On the mount of the Lord it shall be provided.'

And the angel of the Lord called to Abraham a second time from heaven, and said, 'By myself I have sworn,

says the LORD, because you have done this, and have not withheld your son, your only son, I will indeed bless you, and I will multiply your descendants as the stars of heaven and as the sand which is on the seashore. And your descendants shall possess the gate of their enemies, and by your descendants shall all the nations of the earth bless themselves, because you have obeyed my voice.'
Genesis 22.1–18

What is important in this story is that Abraham obeys the voice of God. Through his obedience he worships God, and is rewarded, and the actual sacrifice of the ram shifts to the periphery. Abraham is the father of Judaism, Christianity and Islam.

What gradually changes is the idea that God is revealed, not in nature, but in the events of human history. God requires, not sacrifice, but that we live together in a certain way within society, that we obey God's law, formalized in the Ten Commandments, given to Moses on Mount Sinai. It becomes an ongoing refrain of the prophets that what God desires is mercy, not sacrifice, obedience, not burnt offerings in the temple, as we read in the prophet Isaiah:

'What to me is the multitude of your sacrifices?
    says the LORD;
I have had enough of burnt offerings of rams
    and the fat of fed beasts;
I do not delight in the blood of bulls,
    or of lambs, or of he-goats.

'When you come to appear before me,
     who requires of you
     this tramping of my courts?
Bring no more vain offerings;
     incense is an abomination to me.
New moon and Sabbath and the calling of assemblies –
     I cannot endure iniquity and solemn assembly.
Your new moon and your appointed feasts
     my soul hates;
they have become a burden to me,
     I am weary of bearing them.
When you spread forth your hands,
     I will hide my eyes from you;
even though you make many prayers,
     I will not listen;
     your hands are full of blood.
Wash yourselves; make yourselves clean;
     remove the evil of your doings
     from before my eyes;
cease to do evil,
     learn to do good;
seek justice,
     correct oppression;
defend the fatherless,
     plead for the widow.
Isaiah 1.11–17

This God is not interested in the form of our worship
in the temple, so much as in how we behave towards one

another in the secular world. Worshipping this God puts human beings in a more powerful position, because while we cannot easily change nature, we can change the way we relate to one another in society.

A child who has been well-parented will have been brought to a starting point in language, equipped to go out into the world and engage with others. A child who hasn't been held enough will crave the warmth and comfort of home, and a child who hasn't received sufficient boundaries will crave structure and rules. But a well-parented child will be prepared to leave the safety of home and encounter others who are different. This third stage is characterized by the making of friends and the search for a sexual partner.

Our third imagining of God is embodied in the person of Jesus. Jesus comes out of the Jewish tradition following the law. Already in his own time, however, Jews have begun to interact with others: in the diaspora, Jews are influenced by Greek thought, and Gentiles who worship in their synagogues, but do not keep the law, are called God-fearers. So the question of the relationship between Israel and other peoples is in the air. The Jewish law distinguishes Israel from other nations, Jews from Gentiles, but it creates internal categories as well – clean and unclean, pure and impure, righteous and sinner – and these categories determine the form of relationships possible within Jewish society.

Jesus creates scandal by relating to people to whom he should not relate within the terms of the law. He eats with tax collectors and sinners, touches the sick and the unclean, speaks to Samaritans and Gentiles, and fails to keep the sabbath – he moves outside accepted categories. Adults reach a phase when they are already formed within a particular linguistic tradition, and it is no longer appropriate to demand of them the kind of obedience required of children. At this stage, confronted with real life, adults do not simply apply an external law to decide their response, but make decisions based on conscience, experience and desire. Jesus does what we would take for granted from any master in their field – he experiments, challenges existing categories, and creates something new. He offers, in himself, a new imagining of God.

This God is worshipped through obedience to an inner, individual voice, which comes to maturity in relation to a particular linguistic tradition, but is not ultimately limited by its categories. It is this adult voice that leads us to the limits of our present reality, and expands our imagination. We see this in the story of Peter and Cornelius, in the Acts of the Apostles (the account of what the apostles did after Jesus' death). Cornelius is a devout man, but a Gentile. He hears the voice of God telling him that his prayers have been heard, and that he is to fetch Peter, one of the apostles, to his house in Caesarea. There is already a debate going on in the early Church about whether Gentiles who join must take on the whole of Jewish law and be circumcised, or whether this new imagining of God, embodied in Jesus, takes a different form. Here is Peter telling the Church his story:

'I was in the city of Joppa praying; and in a trance I saw a vision, something descending, like a great sheet, let down from heaven by four corners; and it came down to me. Looking at it closely I observed animals and beasts of prey and reptiles and birds of the air. And I heard a voice saying to me, "Rise, Peter; kill and eat." But I said, "No, Lord; for nothing common or unclean has ever entered my mouth." But the voice answered a second time from heaven, "What God has cleansed you must not call common." This happened three times, and all was drawn up again into heaven. At that very moment three men arrived at the house in which we were, sent to me from Caesarea. And the Spirit told me to go with them, making no distinction. These six brethren also accompanied me, and we entered the man's house. And he told us how he had seen the angel standing in his house and saying, "Send to Joppa and bring Simon called Peter; he will declare to you a message by which you will be saved, you and all your household." As I began to speak, the Holy Spirit fell on them just as on us at the beginning. And I remembered the word of the Lord, how he said, "John baptized with water, but you shall be baptized with the Holy Spirit." If then God gave the same gift to them as he gave to us when we believed in the Lord Jesus Christ, who was I that I could withstand God?' When they heard this they were silenced. And they glorified God, saying, 'Then to the Gentiles also God has granted repentance unto life.'

Acts 11.5–18

God becomes a God in relation to whom previous divisions between people are made obsolete. In relation to this God, there is neither Jew nor Gentile, slave nor free, male nor female. In the evolution of any language, new categories call old categories into question.

What Christianity names is not the end of our need for mother and father God, but the possibility of an adult, friend/lover God corresponding to an adult stage of human development. At this stage, the language we inherit is called into question, and our creative work changes and expands existing categories of language and relationship. Institutions such as democracy in the West, which recognize individual, adult freedoms and rights are the true heirs of this naming.

The movement from mother to friend/lover God is not, however, a simple linear progression, later stages replacing the former, or rendering them obsolete, because every stage is always present. As we grow up, we take in the mothering and fathering we receive, so that these relationships become internal realities. At the same time, we develop our own voice, not simply an application of parental voices, but one that develops out of our individual engagement with the world. In this way, we are three persons in one, and coming to a state of wholeness involves working towards actively loving relationships between these internal figures. This structure of three-in-one also operates at a collective level: an institution such as a hospital, which carries out a predominantly mothering function, taking care of the bodily needs of patients, won't operate very well without good fathering to establish limits and boundaries, and a healthy dose of creative, adult leadership. Nor can these three stages be identified as belonging exclusively to paganism, Judaism or Christianity. We see each stage played out within all the major faith traditions, and in other social contexts as well. Think of the primitive, raw feelings of violence and rage expressed at football matches, or the rule-bound nature of bureaucracy. Important creative breakthroughs keep all human disciplines alive.

What happens in Christianity is the naming of a human possibility that ultimately enables the emergence of the individual as a dominant social form. The fact that this form is now better expressed outside the Church than within it, doesn't alter our need to make this connection, in order to establish where we are now, how we got here, and where we might be headed.

An interpretation is not always correct, and does not represent the analyst telling the patient the truth about herself. The patient must, herself, recognize its truth, in order for it to facilitate healing or change. So an interpretation is more like a move in an ongoing conversation. The patient may reject it straight away, or correct its inaccuracies, or may step inside and inhabit it for awhile, seeing what light it sheds.

My father died just as I was finishing my doctorate in theology. My academic work was deeply tied to my relationship with him. As he was dying from Parkinson's disease, at home in Edinburgh, where he lived in the end with my mother, he was taken care of by district nurses. My friend was also becoming a nurse. It seemed like the right path. I wanted to get away from scholarship, but didn't know where to go.

Within the first month, I knew I couldn't do it. I was in a kind of stupor, paralysed, unable to perform simple tasks. I dropped the course, but continued for a year as an auxiliary, trying to work out what to do.

Looking back, I see that it was grief, and that my father's death had uncovered my relationship with my mother in a new and painful way. I had gone into nursing because I needed to be nursed.

5

The Body of Christ

ॐ

While I was working on my doctorate in Edinburgh, I volunteered, in my spare time, at a project for the homeless across the street from where I lived, run by the Sisters of Mercy, a Roman Catholic religious order. One evening, as I was handing him a dish of food, one of the regulars asked me, 'Are you hungry?' I was taken aback at this role reversal. I was addressing his hunger, not he mine. He held up a plastic bag containing a fish and said, 'I didn't know I would be coming here tonight, so I bought this. Would you like it?' Suddenly I felt very tired and hungry, and I took the fish.

Christianity is easily mistaken as a religion primarily concerned with 'doing good' and 'helping others'. This do-gooding is the more benign version of an impetus to 'save' others, whether they like it or not. In both cases, need is located firmly in the other, who requires either material or spiritual salvation, which it is the Christian's duty to bestow. This reading is quintessentially found in the parable of the Good Samaritan, as often told. In this Sunday School version, it becomes a story about a man who went out of his way to help someone in distress, while others walked by on the other side. The moral of the story seems clear: we should follow the example of the Samaritan and go to the aid of people who need our help. This reading, however, takes no account of the context in which the story is told, or the person to whom Jesus is speaking. The protagonist in the parable is not the Samaritan, but the man who gets beaten up. If we look at the story from his perspective, it immediately becomes more subtle and complex. To do that we have to start further back, and consider why Jesus tells the parable to begin with.

> And behold, a lawyer stood up to put him to the test, saying, 'Teacher, what shall I do to inherit eternal life?' He said to him, 'What is written in the law? How do you read?' And he answered, 'You shall love the Lord your God with all your heart, and with all your soul, and with all your strength, and with all your mind; and your neighbour as yourself.' And he said to him, 'You have answered right; do this, and you will live.'
> *Luke 10.25–28*

Jesus is having a conversation with a lawyer, who is trying to test him. He asks Jesus how to gain eternal life, and Jesus replies by asking what the law says. The lawyer gives the answer written in the law, which Jesus accepts.

> But he, desiring to justify himself, said to Jesus, 'And who is my neighbour?'

Jesus is causing scandal by associating with people with whom the law forbids contact – the sick, the unclean, sinners, Samaritans and Gentiles. His actions are challenging the category 'neighbour' as found in the law. But if Jesus took the path of political correctness, and simply said to the lawyer, 'the Samaritans are also your neighbours', he wouldn't be taking his dilemma seriously. The lawyer's problem is that he cannot imagine the Samaritan, a heretic despised by the Jews, as his neighbour. Recognizing this obstacle, Jesus tells him a story:

> Jesus replied, 'A man was going down from Jerusalem to Jericho, and he fell among robbers, who stripped him and beat him, and departed, leaving him half dead. Now by chance a priest was going down that road; and when he saw him he passed by on the other side. So likewise a Levite, when he came to the place and saw him, passed by on the other side. But a Samaritan, as he journeyed, came to where he was; and when he saw him, he had compassion, and went to him and bound up his wounds, pouring on oil and wine; then he set him on his own beast and brought him to an inn, and took care of him. And the next day he took out two denarii and gave them to the innkeeper, saying, "Take care of him; and whatever more you spend, I will repay you when I come back."'
> *Luke 10.30–35*

In this story, the lawyer is not going to identify with the Samaritan, his enemy, but with the beaten man. Jesus is effectively saying, 'Imagine you are on your way from Jerusalem to Jericho . . .' And it is by imagining himself in a radical state of need, abandoned by those he took to be his neighbours, that the lawyer is able to recognize the Samaritan's actions as those of a true neighbour:

'Which of these three, do you think, proved neighbour to the man who fell among the robbers?' He said, 'The one who showed mercy on him.' And Jesus said to him, 'Go and do likewise.'
Luke 10.36–37

Far from a simple story about helping people in distress, this parable demonstrates how we are limited by the categories of our language, and how our vision can be transformed. What really prevents change is our lack of imagination.

It's always easier to identify lack in others, to think that we know what other people need, or where they're going wrong. Jesus suggests in this parable, however, that only when our own needs are laid bare do we begin to see others clearly. He frequently warns against focusing on lack in others:

Let him who is without sin among you be the first to throw a stone at her.
John 8.7

You hypocrite, first take the log out of your own eye, and then you will see clearly to take the speck out of your brother's eye.
Matthew 7.5

Judge not, that you be not judged.
Matthew 7.1

Until we recognize our own need, we are effectively blind, projecting our own lack outward onto others.

For me, receiving the fish from the homeless man was part of a growing momentum that led me to seek help myself. About a year later, as Lent approached (a six-week preparation for Easter when Roman Catholics traditionally fast), I asked the superior of the Sisters of Mercy in Edinburgh whether, during Lent, I could eat my evening meal with the homeless. She agreed. I didn't tell anyone else what I was doing, including the volunteers giving out the food. It didn't feel like a stunt. I was genuinely going through a difficult time, and it felt like allowing my own need to be made visible, giving up the safe boundary between those who help and those who need, and aligning myself, for once, on the other side. It changed me deeply in that I have never returned to that division. Sometimes someone needs my help, and I give it, and sometimes I need help, and I seek it out.

We all have limited vision, and cannot help but judge what lies outside our vision by the categories we already possess. But in order to move beyond our present limits, we have to allow the possibility that it is our own vision that is deficient, that it is we who are lacking. Judgement is a movement which attempts to define the other by our existing categories, while love is a movement towards the other in relation to whom our categories are called into question, and our own vision expanded.

Let me give an example from art. The art critic Peter Schjeldahl, writing in *The New Yorker*, describes an exhibition of young, established artists at the Museum of Modern Art in Queens. He writes of a painting by the German artist, Neo Rauch: 'I have no idea what the picture is about – Rauch is new to New York, and we are only starting to understand him – but it's riveting.'[1] Here we have the movement of love transcending judgement.

Schjeldahl, an important art critic, doesn't understand what Rauch is doing in the painting – he can't easily place the work within existing categories – but in the face of this strangeness, he doesn't rush to pass judgement – he doesn't say, 'the painting is incoherent', or 'it's a mess'. Instead, he allows that something really new might be emerging in this painting, something which existing categories cannot express, and which will expand and change his own vision.

Within every language, there are the poor. There are those whose existence cannot be described except in terms of what they lack in relation to the dominant vision of success or belonging. Jesus seeks relationship with the outcasts of the law. Our temptation is always to imagine that those who don't conform, are not successful or don't belong are deficient in certain ways. Jesus relates to the outside in such a way as to suggest that it is the dominant vision itself which is lacking, and the governing language which needs to expand. This form of relationship is difficult because it exposes us to our own needs and vulnerabilities in a way that judgement does not. It demands that however much we feel we are in the right, and see the other's limitations

1. Peter Schjeldahl, *The New Yorker*, (4 November 2002), 102–3.

clearly, we allow that it is perhaps we who are blind and limited, unable to apprehend the reality of the person before us. It is a creed of radical openness, drawing us constantly beyond our present limits into relationship with the other, who is never fully known.

It is not that helping others is not part of Jesus' teaching, but he guards against our tendency towards judgement, by asking that in tending the needs of others, we take the role of a servant. After washing the disciples' feet at the last supper, he says to them:

'Do you know what I have done to you? You call me Teacher and Lord; and you are right, for so I am. If I then, your Lord and Teacher, have washed your feet, you also ought to wash one another's feet. For I have given you an example, that you should also do as I have done to you.'
John 13.12–15

A lot of lip service is paid to this injunction, but its meaning is often ignored. A servant is not a person in a position to tell others what their needs are, but someone employed to tend the needs of his master, as his master defines them. In other words, the command is to enter the framework of the other as a servant, accepting the other's own account of their needs, and only from this perspective, to presume to serve.

The duty of a Christian is not to seek out people in distress and prey on their needs, but to wait and prepare for that unexpected encounter with the other that reveals the shape of God by making our own limits clear, and, in so doing, offering a path towards greater wholeness. Like an actor going on stage, once the encounter is upon you, it's too late to prepare. And like the wise and foolish virgins, either you're ready or you're not:

'Then the kingdom of heaven shall be compared to ten maidens who took their lamps and went to meet the bridegroom. Five of them were foolish, and five were wise. For when the foolish took their lamps, they took no oil with them; but the wise took flasks of oil with their lamps. As the bridegroom was delayed, they all slumbered and slept. But at midnight there was a cry, "Behold, the bridegroom! Come out to meet him." Then all those maidens rose and trimmed their lamps. And the foolish said to the wise, "Give us some of your oil, for our lamps are going out." But the wise replied, "Perhaps there will not be enough for us and for you; go rather to the dealers and buy for yourselves." And while they went to buy, the bridegroom came, and those who were ready went in with him to the marriage feast; and the door was shut. Afterward the other maidens came also, saying, "Lord, lord, open to us." But he replied, "Truly, I say to you, I do not know you." Watch therefore, for you know neither the day nor the hour.'
Matthew 25.1–13

In the Christian tradition, there is something irreducibly unexpected and mysterious about encountering Christ in the other. The other remains, in a deep sense, unknown;

not contained within our limited categories. It is the nature of our response in this encounter that matters, our ability to recognize, in the other, an image of full humanity. In the Parable of the Last Judgement, this quality of recognition is what separates the righteous from sinners:

'When the Son of man comes in his glory, and all the angels with him, then he will sit on his glorious throne. Before him will be gathered all the nations, and he will separate them one from another as a shepherd separates the sheep from the goats, and he will place the sheep at his right hand, but the goats at the left. Then the King will say to those at his right hand, "Come, O blessed of my Father, inherit the kingdom prepared for you from the foundation of the world; for I was hungry and you gave me food, I was thirsty and you gave me drink, I was a stranger and you welcomed me, I was sick and you visited me, I was in prison and you came to me." Then the righteous will answer him, "Lord, when did we see you hungry and feed thee, or thirsty and give thee drink? And when did we see thee sick or in prison and visit thee?" And the King will answer them, "Truly, I say to you, as you did it to one of the least of these my brethren, you did it to me." Then he will say to those at his left hand, "Depart from me, you cursed, into the eternal fire prepared for the devil and his angels; for I was hungry and you gave me no food, I was thirsty and you gave me no drink, I was a stranger and you did not welcome me, naked and you did not clothe me, sick and in prison and

you did not visit me." Then they also will answer, "Lord, when did we see thee hungry or thirsty or a stranger or naked or sick or in prison, and did not minister to thee?" Then he will answer them, "Truly, I say to you, as you did it not to one of the least of these, you did it not to me." And they will go away into eternal punishment, but the righteous into eternal life.'
Matthew 25.31–46

This is not a parable about meeting or failing to meet targets; solving the homelessness problem, the housing problem or overcrowding in prisons. It's not about categories of people who have problems we're trying to solve. It's not offering a general law about homelessness, poverty or the prison system. The strange thing about this parable is that neither the righteous nor the sinners know who they are. Both ask, *When did we meet you?* The parable is about our ability to recognize, in the particular encounters that come our way, our own humanity in the other. This meeting is at once human and divine, it moves us beyond our present limits, creating new relationship, and leading us more deeply into communion with the wholeness we seek to realize, both in ourselves and in the world at large.

It's no mistake that the body of Christ becomes the dominant image in Christianity. The body is the site of interpersonal encounter, which, in Christianity, becomes a new location of relationship with God. This movement from collective obedience to individual response, enacted by Jesus, sets the foundation for the emergence of the individual as a dominant social form. It's a mistake, however, to imagine that this development replaces the need for law-abiding, collective action. Jesus himself says:

'Think not that I have come to abolish the law and the prophets; I have come not to abolish them but to fulfil them. For truly, I say to you, till heaven and earth pass away, not an iota, not a dot, will pass from the law until all is accomplished.'
Matthew 5.17–18

What Jesus embodies is a paradoxical tension with the law: you must obey the law until and unless you must break it. Breaking the law may be prophetic, or it may simply be criminal or insane. Only time will tell. How many people whom we now consider leaders or creative geniuses ahead of their time were once dismissed, rejected, imprisoned or even killed? New developments which, to begin with, seem incomprehensible, outrageous, a complete break with the status quo, gradually become part of the law and are taken for granted. What is really new can only be discerned against the backdrop of existing language.

In order for the law to remain alive, there needs to be a lived tension between the collective action by which it is obeyed and passed on, and the engagement of individuals which challenges, expands and renews it. Without this tension, creative life comes to a halt. When no change is permitted, or when it is heavily legislated from the centre, allowing no scope for individual creativity, the law becomes the dead repetition of history. When the law is abandoned, there is no backdrop against which change can be discerned, no common palate, so individual action has no real impact.

I didn't start thinking about myself as a Roman Catholic until I was 16 and we were living at the theological research institute in Jerusalem. What prompted this self-reflection was the fact that everyone kept asking me what church I belonged to. I had grown up simply calling myself a Christian. My parents had left the Roman Catholic Church but hadn't joined any other, so that left me and my brother in a kind of limbo. I had been confirmed Roman Catholic through my school, but, for me, this was just one event in an extremely ecumenical form of religious practice, which did not, in itself, create any great sense of institutional belonging. It was the need to identify myself to others, who clearly did not share my culture, that really got me thinking.

When the early Church decided that Gentiles who joined would not be required to follow the whole of Jewish law, or be circumcised, they were creating a very complex issue about belonging. Whether or not Jews accepted Jesus as the Messiah, they were familiar with messianic language. Hope for and belief in the coming of a Messiah is part of the Jewish story, the shape of an imagined future, and Jesus was not the only figure to attract such claims. How, then, to convey the significance of Jesus, the difference he embodied, to people who did not share this collective backdrop? In some ways, this problem is very similar to one we face today: How do you have a conversation with someone from a different culture, with whom you share no common language? How do you communicate what's important or what's new? How do you tell a joke without an assumed palette of meaning and reference?

Christians eventually solved this problem by appropriating the categories of their audience, using Greek thought to articulate the meaning of Jesus, turning him into a more cosmic figure than would have been permitted within the terms of Jewish narrative. With the collapse of the Roman Empire, the Church became the imperial structure, the dominant, governing power enforcing the centre, not living at the edge. Becoming a ruling force ducked the real question of how to create relationship without a common language, and turned Christianity into a language of oppression. But the story of Jesus has its own power, so while Christians ruled, Christians also opposed this rule, and Christian history is a complex interweaving of many strands, often in opposition to each other.

The question that Christianity poses remains alive today: if all people are loved equally by God, what implications does this have for how we relate to each other, and how can this love be expressed without eliminating the differences that make us who we are? I think the answer is sex.

The law, understood as all systems of shared language that govern the way we live together and communicate in society, is passed on and enforced through parental structures – by parents in the home and by parental institutions such as schools and the justice system. These structures communicate language primarily in one direction, from parent to child. They are the means by which children are furnished with the tools required to live in human society, and by which both children and adults are kept in order. If, as an adult, I again become a student, I put myself, structurally speaking, in a child-like position, taking in the language offered in order to learn. Parent to child is the structure of a certain form of social relationship.

Sex is another form: the form of an encounter between two adults in which both already possess language. The task here, is not for one to transmit language to the other, or judge the other, but for both to enter into conversation. In a parent–child structure, the focus is on the child's development and successful entry into language. In a sexual structure, the goal is to create a common space, a single body formed through the coming together of different bodies. This is an enormously difficult task because the other is different to me, and conversation of this kind requires work. This is the form of relationship that pertains between lovers, but also between friends and in adult to adult structures, such as democracy.

Political correctness is an idolatrous worship of difference for its own sake. Under its banner, identity becomes a weapon of difference; sex, a sign of weakness. In a sexual structure, difference takes us to the point of encounter, but the encounter itself requires an openness to the other, enabling the creation of a child; the permutation of difference into a new, shared reality, greater than the sum of its parts. For this encounter to work, we must allow our own identity to be transformed.

What if Jesus' teaching can be read, not primarily in a

parent to child voice, but in the adult to adult voice of a good sex guide? In this encounter with the other, Jesus advises, don't judge, don't simply bring your own categories to bear. Instead, take the role of a servant – try to understand the other person by entering into their framework, engaging with their categories. Be prepared to forgive. We are all caught up in patterns of dysfunctional behaviour, and although this might not eliminate individual responsibility, it means that often the only way out of destructive cycles of relationship is to offer a new beginning, even when seemingly undeserved.

In Jerusalem, I did end up calling myself a Roman Catholic, because that was the form of Christianity I recognized. And yet, the tradition I had inherited from my parents was to be a Roman Catholic in rebellion. It took a lot longer to work out what this meant for me, and how I wanted to position myself in the struggle.

What I came to see is that while my parents had rejected the parental structure of the Church, they hadn't rejected the story. They were able to separate out the form of authority delivering the story from the rich and varied narrative of human searching which, they felt, it was corrupting.

They were like musicians raised in a totalitarian regime whose leader has to approve all the scores, dying to play their own music, and exceptionally well-equipped to do so. Without my being aware of it at the time, I was given an incredible and unusual formation in the liturgy and tradition of the Roman Catholic Church, without the oppressive exercise of parental authority found inside the

Church itself. This put me in a unique position in relation to my peers. The parents of most of my Roman Catholic friends had either left the Church altogether, and with it any real connection to the tradition, or had remained in the desultory mood of bored and critical teenagers – not an inspiring position for their children. What my parents claimed was their right, as competent adults, to make a contribution. In this spirit, they conducted an exciting and creative exploration of the possibilities of Christian life in a sexual, rather than parental, mode.

The results of this investigation were not always successful – on an emotional level it was often disastrous, since they had not developed any language to express their inner world, and had very little self-awareness. But, in other ways, it was thrilling. Their approach placed us inside the story, so that instead of repeating dead history, I had the sense of participating in a living narrative to which I would, in turn, contribute.

The widespread abandonment of Christianity in the West seems to me primarily a rejection of its parental structure, and the inability to gain any independent access to the tradition outside this form. My own experience working with community groups and undergraduates suggests that the search for meaning is strong, as is the desire to engage with a collective narrative. The question that remains, therefore, is what might a post-Church form of worship look like?

6

With My Body I Thee Worship

❦

At a certain moment in my process, I began, every evening, to write a list of everyone I had encountered in the course of the day. I didn't write anything about the encounter, just the name of the person, or a brief description if I didn't know their name. I included anyone with whom I had had an exchange, in whatever medium. I continued this practice for about six months.

Worship, in the story I have told, takes three forms: first, sacrifice, the powerful outward projection of internal realities, both individual and collective, onto an object in the external world, who is made to carry the burden of what properly belongs to us. Jesus, in these terms, is a sacrifice, taking on the sins of the world. We see, in the overwhelming grief expressed at the death of Princess Diana, a sacrificial form of response. Identification with sports teams and celebrities also comes within this form.

Obeying the law, the second form of worship, turns away from sacrifice. The law is a demystification of sacrifice; the difference between idolizing a pop star and taking music lessons yourself. Through the law, human beings assume a new level of conscious agency in the creation of their world.

Sex is the third stage. Here, an individual formed by the law relates to the law, no longer as an obedient child, but as an equal, and through a process of encounter, new possibilities arise. Here, also, is the encounter of different laws, the meeting of adults who all possess language, and must converse in order to create common space.

An unformed child is spontaneous, because she, as yet, lacks the limitations and inhibitions language will bring. An adult who has internalized the law, however, reaches a spontaneity achieved through language itself. Think of a musician who has mastered their instrument and is able, as a result, to improvise and create.

It seems to me that each new stage in the story goes through all these forms; that the whole process of incarnation, word becoming flesh, is a never-ending, spiral-shaped outworking of these three stages, so that when we reach the end of one cycle, we begin again and yet are in a different place.

I would characterize the present situation in the West as an in-between stage – the end of our worship of Jesus as God in human form, and the beginning of a new cycle exploring how our human form, in light of Jesus, leads us into God. Worship of Jesus begins as an overwhelming sense of his importance, becomes institutionalized and legalized in the parental structure of the Church. Then, when the parents won't let go, it is rejected and the rights of adulthood asserted – democracy, freedom, equality, sex. This adulthood, however, is not wholly other to the tradition that precedes it, but its very fruit.

Sex is a powerful symbol in our present society. Images of sex are everywhere, in every medium, in all our public spaces. We are in the first stage of this new form, projecting our sexual desires outward and experiencing them externally in the world around us. It's no accident that the Christian Churches are completely preoccupied with sex at the moment. They rightly sense the threat our sexual freedom presents to their parental structures of authority. Our task is to begin naming this new form in order to gain a more conscious ability to act within it, to understand sex as a form of social relationship, distinct from a parental structure.

When I started writing my list of daily encounters, it wasn't the application of a theory, so much as an instinct about where I needed to go. I adopted this discipline, then began reflecting on what it means.

One of the big obstacles to social change is the widespread feeling that nothing we do makes any difference, that it's impossible to act to effect change. It's not that we don't know what kind of world we'd like to live in – a world in which peace and justice reign, and everyone has access to the basic necessities of life, including healthcare and education, and in which we live in harmony with the natural world, safeguarding the future of the planet. This is a vision on which we probably all agree. And yet, we are bombarded on all sides with stories of the disasters facing us

– conflicts around the world, terrorism, poverty, injustice, global warming. The gap between where we are and where we'd like to be seems immense and unbridgeable, and in the face of it, it's easy to conclude that there's nothing we can do; to retreat into a blinkered private life, leaving the problem for others to solve.

But while our mind is overwhelmed by this relentless reporting on the world's problems, creating hopelessness and apathy, our body is firmly rooted to the ground, locating us in time and space, and defining for us a limited sphere of action.

If we think of the body, not as an inert physical object, but as the form of the self in relationship, then finding the limits of the self involves developing awareness of the web of relationality, both internal and external, that makes us up. My discipline of recording my daily encounters was about exploring the limits of my world, and, within those limits, embracing the unexpected, letting the world talk back to me, and noticing what I might otherwise miss or take for granted. Our mind easily imagines that we have no limits, while our body defines where we begin and end. And without limits, we cannot act.

Finding the edges of my world enables me to live inside it more precisely. That doesn't mean that the edges don't change – new people arrive, others depart; the boundary is flexible but present. But it is within this world only that I have both the ability and the power to act. While I may maintain an awareness of the global scene, I preserve my imaginative and bodily energy for the work that is mine to do. Having limits means letting some things in, and keeping others out.

Relationships are a creative work, the form of our connection to the world. But they are also limited. I cannot have a relationship with the world at large, but only with particular people, institutions, and communities. These connections may indeed cross the planet, but they do so on particular trajectories. If I concentrate on the world's problems in general, but fail to inhabit my own skin, I make myself powerless.

Part of our powerlessness, it seems to me, is that we are oppressed by a sense of obligation, by the feeling that we ought to be doing things we are failing to do: going to the gym more often, being better to our friends, spending more time with the children, working harder, working less hard. Inhabiting this world more fully may seem a dismal prospect. But concentrating on what we think we ought to do is not a route to greater embodiment, so much as the imposition of a controlling mind upon our bodily reality.

Coming to know our body and its limits involves letting go of this controlling mind and exploring how we actually feel and what we really desire; entering into relationship with the unknown and the forbidden within ourselves.

One could argue that depth psychology is a secular development of the confessional. The confessional requires people to own up to their inner world, and acknowledge the darker side, but to do so in the context of a language of sin and judgement. I may admit to hating my neighbour, but I must promise to try to stop hating him in order to be forgiven. This communicates a very powerful sense that we should not be feeling what we truly are feeling, and leads to a great deal of repression and denial. We may have ditched the confessional, but this kind of self-judgement abounds.

Depth psychology provides another path which involves cultivating an awareness of how we feel, without judgement. This requires the ability to distinguish feelings from a decision to act on them. I cannot allow myself fully to experience the hatred, rage and envy that may make me want to stab my neighbour and cut her up in little pieces, cannot think about its meaning for me, unless I know that my feelings are not going to lead directly to action. Respecting this distance between how we feel and how we act is a prerequisite for self-knowledge.

How boring, you might imagine. Is life just one long process of self-reflection? Is there no spontaneity, no meeting of action and desire without pre-meditation? The romantic fantasy of falling in love and living happily ever after relentlessly pursues us; the vision of a world without original sin. Given that we are all implicated in patterns of dysfunction, however, the reality is that relationships take work, and self-knowledge is a necessary task. In a sense, we need to become disembodied before we attain real embodiment.

During the first year of my PhD studies in Edinburgh, I developed severe writer's block, felt paralysed and unable to proceed. My intuition was that I needed to dance. A friend pointed me in the direction of a local studio, and I started classes. At first, I hated seeing myself in the mirror and my regard was full of self-judgement. I didn't look as I felt I ought to look and my body didn't seem a real expression of my self. I felt trapped inside, dying to get out.

Language dislocates us. Chucked out of the Garden of Eden, we are forced to inhabit a world constructed in human terms with all the suffering and dysfunction that brings. Language can disconnect us from our bodies – taking our mind in one direction, our body in another. We also guard against unbearable feelings by escaping into the mind. At the same time, we are capable of finding, through our human struggle, a new kind of wholeness and embodiment, a spontaneity that greets us on the other side.

I have now been dancing for 12 years, and usually it's in a studio without mirrors. But when I catch a glimpse of myself, or see myself on film, I have a different reaction. It's not that I'm now everything I would have liked, but that I look at myself and say, 'that's me'. I recognize myself with compassion and humour, and even respect. I have greater acceptance of my limits, and delight at where my body, as an instrument, can take me.

I have a friend who talks a lot more than I do. I'm a person who needs quite a lot of space and silence. And yet, we are drawn to friendship with each other. When I need silence, I have to tell her to be quiet for awhile or else I couldn't go on with the relationship. But because we are open about these limits, and have come to know and understand our different needs, we can also be close friends.

If we worshipped our differences, rather than the friendship itself, I would not be able to tell her to be quiet, and she would not feel free to speak and, as a result, we would not get along. If I assumed a position of judgement and told her that she talks too much, I would be trying to eliminate her difference, make her more like me. Instead we chart a path that allows our differences, moderated to respect the constraints of our mutuality. When we veer too far off course, this creates a tension that pulls us back.

We all share one planet with limited resources and cannot, therefore, avoid a conversation about how to live together. This conversation brings us face to face with seemingly intractable differences. How often do we approach these differences either with judgement, or with worshipful respect, avoiding, in both cases, real conversation?

My brother and I have a turbulent relationship – a powerful hate/love mix defines our encounters. The reasons for this go way back, stemming from factors in our parents' relationship that determined the different roles we played. We are capable of descending into well-worn patterns of mutually destructive behaviour. In recent years, however, we have become much better at recognizing when this is about to occur, and agreeing not to go there. We have learned, through endless repetition, that we will never solve our problems through the blame and recrimination, the recitation of our history that we are so tempted to enact.

We cannot function in our day-to-day lives, or as a society, without making judgements. But we are always tempted to regard these judgements as closed and absolute, believing that we are right and others are to blame; that in the same position, we would not have acted so. The refusal to judge is a refusal to ignore the possibility that we are wrong. It demands that we maintain a paradoxical tension with the law: while we cannot avoid judging, our judgements are never final.

Forgiveness is a willingness to allow a new beginning, not ignoring past injustice, but accepting that it may never be fully resolved. It requires recognition that we are all implicated in patterns of destructive and dysfunctional relationship, and that present conflicts often have histories going back generations. The only way forward may be to take responsibility for our own part, and agree to move on.

Forgiving an individual who has wronged us may be unbearably difficult, and take considerable time, but, it too, is a recognition that we are all fallible and will all need forgiveness in turn.

The real alternative to advertising is not a dull and self-righteous moral rectitude that denies the pleasure and importance of the material world, but a form of storytelling that charts a real course between where we are now and the possibilities that exist for human fulfilment and transformation. This discipline requires that we attend closely to our present reality, and cultivate, in hope, an expectation of where it may lead.

What goes on, at least in a Roman Catholic Church, is called 'liturgy', which derives from the Greek meaning 'public work'. It's essentially a form of storytelling. Throughout the year, the whole story of Jesus' birth, life, teaching, death and resurrection is retold. The idea is that through the telling of the story, which engages the whole body, and all the seasons of the year, we become part of the story ourselves. The down side is that the power structure of the Church dictates what can and cannot happen in the story, which leads to a lot of endless repetition of the same. But the approach is interesting.

Story, as a social structure, is different from law. Law judges each new development in terms of existing categories. Morality, for example, is a legal codification of behaviour. The Church is all worked up about sex because present patterns of sexual behaviour don't fit the code. Law presumes that the future will be like the present, until proven otherwise. Social sciences, for example, make their predictions based on this assumption. In a narrative structure, however, the future depends on what we do. The possibility exists that our actions will create a new reality, bringing the story to a new chapter.

Much action is stifled because we think of it in legal instead of narrative terms. There is a sense that we cannot and should not act unless we know what the outcome of our action will be, and insure against all eventualities. We criticize public figures when things turn out differently from promised, or when unintended consequences arise. We demand compensation, threaten litigation, and want to hold people to account for any unforeseen occurrence. As a result, we are completely paralysed and unable to take risks.

Deciding how to act in a story is different than it is in a legal structure. In a legal framework one is asking, *How should I act, given how everybody else acts, and how I am expected to act in this situation?* In a story, one is concerned with plot, *How should I act, given what has happened so far, and where I think this story is going?* What is our story? The advertising that dominates our public space would have us think that there is no shared story, that our society is made up purely of private narratives of personal choice. Action, in these terms, extends no further than selecting the right shampoo.

Whether we like it or not, the story of Christianity is the story that has dominated in the West. The West is incomprehensible without this story. Does this mean that we should all become Christian and return to church? No. Does it mean that no other stories should be allowed into our public space? No. It means that the story we are part of is not simply of our choosing. This is true on a personal level as well. Many factors about my story are entirely out of my control – who my parents are, where I was born, my mother tongue. Our collective story has this same degree of immutability.

We have tried to overcome the problem of religious conflict by leaving our collective stories out of the public domain, and instead, basing our conversation about collective life on what all nice people would do. As a result our political life is dominated by a legal structure disconnected from any narrative tradition, so that we experience politics as an endless repetition of the same, and reduction to the lowest common denominator, with no form of action able to lead us to the next stage of our tale. At the same time, the only images of human fulfilment available to all of us are those of advertising, which implicitly deny the possibility of collective action by selling us a story of private choice, lining the coffers of the private sector.

Narrative is, in fact, much more tolerant of difference than law. Religious conflict is based on asserting the supremacy of one narrative over another, and on the attempt of religious authorities to control the narrative flow. But narrative, separated from oppressive structures, has the potential to enable action where legal structures paralyse. In a narrative, differences may interweave, there may be many plot lines and characters. Different communities form narrative relationships, which do not eliminate their difference, but allow them to inhabit a common world.

When I was 13, a Jewish colleague of my father asked if I would become a regular babysitter for his son, then aged three. His mother had, for reasons which remained unknown to me, deserted the family, and his father felt that his son needed another stable presence in his life. They lived around the corner from us, so we were also neighbours. I felt very honoured to be asked, and accepted. For ten years I babysat this child. When I was older, I sometimes stayed at the house and looked after him when his father was away. In this time, the father remarried and his new wife also had a child, a daughter from a first marriage. The family were observant – they kept kosher and went to synagogue. The little boy attended a Jewish school. He was fascinated by the fact that I was not Jewish, and, to begin with, frequently asked me if I was, continually surprised at my reply. I learned how to operate in a kosher kitchen, and if I was babysitting on Shabbat, the little boy would lead the prayers. As he approached 13, I listened to him practising his Torah portion, and at his Bar Mitzvah, I was as proud as any Jewish mother. It never occurred to me that he should become Christian, or I Jewish. Our difference was part of our common tale.

When I say that we need to reconnect with Christianity as the dominant story in the West, I don't mean that the Christian story should dominate. I mean that we cannot understand how we got here without reference to this story. But the story we now need to tell must encompass the dark side of our tale, the violence perpetrated in the name of the Church, and the reasons why people abandoned the narrative altogether. All kinds of things happen in a story, the whole range of human possibility, both light and dark. If we were able to name this darker side as part of us, we might find ourselves able to own the story once again, and discover our way forward in it.

If we separate the story from the institutions that have tried to control it, what Christianity offers, it seems to me, is a way of creating a common narrative without eliminating difference. The path Jesus offers doesn't say what the story should be, but suggests how we might relate to each other in order to create the kind of relationships that bring about true peace and friendship. The story is up to us, the future unknown and undetermined, rich with possibility, pregnant with hope.

Acknowledgements

Thanks to Giles Semper, who invited me to write this book, to Christine Smith and all at SCM-Canterbury Press who brought it to fruition. Thanks to the friends, colleagues and mentors who read the manuscript in draft, and provided important critical feedback: Alex Crowe, Thomas Kemple, Nicholas Postlethwaite, Mark White, Anne McHugh, Zenon Bankowski (also for our work together on the parables), Patty Burgess, John Halsey, Christopher Irvine, Yvon Bonenfant, Lisa Marie Russo, Eva Casson-du Mont, Elinor Newman, Mary Clare Foa, Gaby Agis, Lizzie LeQuesne, Paul Bayley, Anita Rosada and William Young. Thanks to my Advisory Committee for their active support (members not already named): Nikki Crane, Brendan McCarthy, Richard McLaren, Bob O'Dell, Mehul Shah, and Brendan Walsh. Thanks to the late Peter Askonas for his unflagging interest and support, and to Sylvia for her generous hospitality. Thanks to Tom Devonshire Jones for his wisdom and counsel. Thanks to Jean and Bob Cincotta, Mary Ann Holthaus and all my well-wishers in their circle. Thanks to my parents, Charles

Davis and Florence Henderson Davis (both now dead), who, by risking the unknown, created possibilities for new forms of life. Thanks to my brother, Anthony Davis, for his astute engagement with my work, and so much else. And thanks to AF, for more than I can name.